Cat Hen Duck Goose Dog

Pig Goat Cow Cat Hen Duck

D

Goose Dog Sheep Pig Goat Cow

Cat Hen Duck Goose Dog Sheep

Pig Goat Cow Cat Hen  Duck

Fiddle-I-Fee

Fiddle-I-Fee

A Farmyard Song for the Very Young

Adapted and illustrated by Melissa Sweet

JOY STREET BOOKS
Little, Brown and Company
Boston   Toronto   London

First Edition

Library of Congress Cataloging-in-Publication Data

Sweet, Melissa.
  Fiddle-I-fee : a farmyard song for the very young / [Melissa
Sweet]. — 1st ed.
    p.   cm.
  Summary: In this cumulative nursery rhyme and folk song,
a parade forms when several farm animals join a boy on his
journey around the farmyard.
  ISBN 0-316-82516-6
  1. Folk-songs, American — Texts.   2. Children's songs,
American — Texts.   3. Nursery rhymes, American.
4. Children's poetry, American.   [1. Domestic animals —
Songs and music.   2. Folk songs, American.   3. Nursery
rhymes.]   I. Title.
PZ8.3.S99518Fi   1992
782.42162'13'00833 — dc20   90-40884

Joy Street Books are published by
Little, Brown and Company (Inc.)

10   9   8   7   6   5   4   3   2   1

WOR

Published simultaneously in Canada
by Little, Brown & Company (Canada) Limited

Printed in the United States of America

to
Abbe

I had a cat
and the cat pleased me,
I fed my cat under yonder tree;

Cat went fiddle-i-fee.

I had a . . .

hen

and the hen pleased me,
I fed my hen under yonder tree;
Hen went chipsy-chopsy,

Cat went fiddle-i-fee.

I had a . . .

 **duck**
and the duck pleased me,
I fed my duck under yonder tree;
Duck went quack, quack,

Hen went chipsy-chopsy,
Cat went fiddle-i-fee.

I had a . . .

**goose**
and the goose pleased me,
I fed my goose under yonder tree;
Goose went swishy-swashy,

Duck went quack, quack,
Hen went chipsy-chopsy,
Cat went fiddle-i-fee.

I had a . . .

dog
and the dog pleased me,
I fed my dog under yonder tree;
Dog went bow-wow, bow-wow,

Goose went swishy-swashy,
Duck went quack, quack,
Hen went chipsy-chopsy,
Cat went fiddle-i-fee.

I had a . . .

sheep

and the sheep pleased me,
I fed my sheep under yonder tree;
Sheep went baa, baa,

Dog went bow-wow, bow-wow,
Goose went swishy-swashy,
Duck went quack, quack,
Hen went chipsy-chopsy,
Cat went fiddle-i-fee.

I had a . . .

pig

and the pig pleased me,
I fed my pig under yonder tree;
Pig went griffy-gruffy,

Sheep went baa, baa,
Dog went bow-wow, bow-wow,
Goose went swishy-swashy,
Duck went quack, quack,
Hen went chipsy-chopsy,
Cat went fiddle-i-fee.

I had a . . .

**goat**

and the goat pleased me,
I fed my goat under yonder tree;
Goat went bleat, bleat,

Pig went griffy-gruffy,
Sheep went baa, baa,
Dog went bow-wow, bow-wow,
Goose went swishy-swashy,
Duck went quack, quack,
Hen went chipsy-chopsy,
Cat went fiddle-i-fee.

I had a . . .

COW

and the cow pleased me,
I fed my cow under yonder tree;
Cow went moo, moo . . .

Goat went bleat, bleat,
Pig went griffy-gruffy,
sheep went baa, baa,
Dog went bow-wow, bow-wow,
Goose went swishy-swashy,

Duck went quack, quack,
Hen went chipsy-chopsy,
Cat went . . .

fiddle

Fiddle-I-Fee

Traditional
Arranged by Alain Mallet

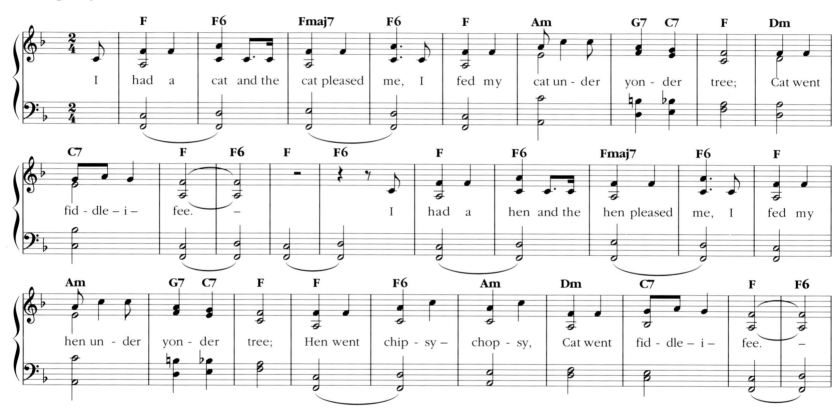

I had a cat and the cat pleased me, I fed my cat un-der yon-der tree; Cat went fid-dle-i- fee. — I had a hen and the hen pleased me, I fed my hen un-der yon-der tree; Hen went chip-sy- chop-sy, Cat went fid-dle-i- fee. —

I had a duck and the duck pleased me, I fed my duck un - der yon - der tree;

Duck went quack, quack, Hen went chip - sy - chop - sy, Cat went fid - dle - i - fee. —

Cat Hen Duck Goose Dog  Sheep

 Pig Goat Cow Cat Hen Duck

Goose Dog Sheep  Pig Goat Cow

Cat Hen  Duck Goose Dog Sheep

Pig Goat Cow Cat Hen  Duck